D1518276

COOL CATS

Norwegian Forest Cats

by Domini Brown

BELLWETHER MEDIA • MINNEAPOLIS, MN

BLASTOFF!
2
READERS

Note to Librarians, Teachers, and Parents:

Blastoff! Readers are carefully developed by literacy experts and combine standards-based content with developmentally appropriate text.

Level 1 provides the most support through repetition of high-frequency words, light text, predictable sentence patterns, and strong visual support.

Level 2 offers early readers a bit more challenge through varied simple sentences, increased text load, and less repetition of high-frequency words.

Level 3 advances early-fluent readers toward fluency through increased text and concept load, less reliance on visuals, longer sentences, and more literary language.

Level 4 builds reading stamina by providing more text per page, increased use of punctuation, greater variation in sentence patterns, and increasingly challenging vocabulary.

Level 5 encourages children to move from "learning to read" to "reading to learn" by providing even more text, varied writing styles, and less familiar topics.

Whichever book is right for your reader, Blastoff! Readers are the perfect books to build confidence and encourage a love of reading that will last a lifetime!

This edition first published in 2017 by Bellwether Media, Inc.

No part of this publication may be reproduced in whole or in part without written permission of the publisher. For information regarding permission, write to Bellwether Media, Inc., Attention: Permissions Department, 5357 Penn Avenue South, Minneapolis, MN 55419.

Library of Congress Cataloging-in-Publication Data

Names: Brown, Domini, author.
Title: Norwegian Forest Cats / by Domini Brown.
Other titles: Blastoff! Readers. 2, Cool Cats.
Description: Minneapolis, MN : Bellwether Media, Inc., [2017] | Series:
   Blastoff readers. Cool Cats | Audience: Ages 5-8. | Audience: K to grade 3.
   | Includes bibliographical references and index.
Identifiers: LCCN 2015049321 | ISBN 9781626173972 (hardcover : alk. paper)
Subjects: LCSH: Norwegian forest cat–Juvenile literature. | Cat
   breeds–Juvenile literature.
Classification: LCC SF449.N65 B76 2017 | DDC 636.8/3–dc23
LC record available at http://lccn.loc.gov/2015049321

Printed in the United States of America, North Mankato, MN.

Table of Contents

What Are Norwegian Forest Cats?

Norwegian forest cats are large and **hardy**.

The long-haired **breed** is known for its thick fur.

5

Their name can be shortened to Wegie. It sounds like "wee-gee."

In Norway, the cats are called
skogkatt. This means "forest cat"
in Norwegian!

History of Norwegian Forest Cats

Wegies are the **official** cat of Norway.

Norway

N
W · E
S

They have lived in cold Norwegian lands for hundreds of years.

The cats may have first come to North America with **Vikings** in the early 1000s.

They traveled with Vikings and hunted mice on their ships.

In 1979, the first pair of modern Wegies came to the United States.

The breed is a favorite among cat lovers today!

Wegies have a lot of hair.
Soft **ruffs** surround their
triangle-shaped heads.

14

Norwegian Forest Cat Profile

— fluffy tail

— ear tufts

— triangle-shaped head

— neck ruff

Weight: 9 to 16 pounds (4 to 7 kilograms)

Life Span: 14 to 16 years

Tufts of long fur grow from their ears and feet. Their tails are big and fluffy.

Their **coats** are often **tabby** or **tortoiseshell**. Some have **solid** coats.

Norwegian Forest Cat Coats

solid

tabby

bi-color

tortoiseshell

Once a year, Wegies lose their **undercoat**. Then their fur is thinner for summer.

Watchful and Calm

Wegies have strong bodies. They are good climbers and like to be up high.

They watch people and other animals from above.

Norwegian forest cats **adapt** well to change. They are calm and not easily bothered.

This makes them excellent cats
for families with young children!

Glossary

adapt—to get used to new things or surroundings

breed—a type of cat

coats—the hair or fur covering some animals

hardy—able to live through difficult conditions

official—publicly known

ruffs—areas of longer fur around the necks of some animals

solid—one color

tabby—a pattern that has stripes, patches, or swirls of another color

tortoiseshell—a pattern of yellow, orange, and black with few or no patches of white

tufts—small bunches of hairs

undercoat—a layer of short fur underneath an outer layer of longer fur

Vikings—a group of people from Denmark, Norway, and Sweden that attacked the coasts of Europe between the years of 800 and 1000

To Learn More

AT THE LIBRARY

Cuddy, Robbin. *Learn to Draw Cats & Kittens: Step-by-Step Instructions for More Than 25 Favorite Feline Friends.* Lake Forest, Calif.: Walter Foster Publishing, 2016.

Furstinger, Nancy. *Norwegian Forest Cats.* Edina, Minn.: Abdo Pub., 2006.

Sexton, Colleen. *The Life Cycle of a Cat.* Minneapolis, Minn.: Bellwether Media, 2011.

ON THE WEB
Learning more about Norwegian forest cats is as easy as 1, 2, 3.

1. Go to www.factsurfer.com.

2. Enter "Norwegian forest cats" into the search box.

3. Click the "Surf" button and you will see a list of related web sites.

With factsurfer.com, finding more information is just a click away.

Index

The images in this book are reproduced through the courtesy of: Eric Isselee, front cover, pp. 13, 15; Jan Faukner, p. 4; Joanna22, p. 5; Elisa Putti, p. 6; Astrid Gast, pp. 7, 9, 10, 16; Julia Remezova, p. 8; Waldemar Dabrowski, p. 11; Petra Wegner/ Alamy, p. 12; Kaisa Savolainen, p. 14; Cartela, p. 17 (top left); HHelene, pp. 17 (top right), 19; Linn Currie, p. 17 (bottom left); digitalienspb, p. 17 (bottom right); blickwinkel/ kucka/ Alamy, p. 18; Juniors Bildarchiv/ F215/ Alamy, p. 20; Heather Katz/ SuperStock, p.21 (subject); zastolskiy Victor, p. 21 (background).